Jean Marcel Mbikayi Mpanya

Introduction to tutorial design with HyperCard

AF671805

Jean Marcel Mbikayi Mpanya

Introduction to tutorial design with HyperCard

ScienciaScripts

Imprint
Any brand names and product names mentioned in this book are subject to trademark, brand or patent protection and are trademarks or registered trademarks of their respective holders. The use of brand names, product names, common names, trade names, product descriptions etc. even without a particular marking in this work is in no way to be construed to mean that such names may be regarded as unrestricted in respect of trademark and brand protection legislation and could thus be used by anyone.

Cover image: www.ingimage.com

This book is a translation from the original published under ISBN 978-620-6-70860-5.

Publisher:
Sciencia Scripts
is a trademark of
Dodo Books Indian Ocean Ltd. and OmniScriptum S.R.L publishing group

120 High Road, East Finchley, London, N2 9ED, United Kingdom
Str. Armeneasca 28/1, office 1, Chisinau MD-2012, Republic of Moldova, Europe
Printed at: see last page
ISBN: 978-620-8-26870-1

Copyright © Jean Marcel Mbikayi Mpanya
Copyright © 2024 Dodo Books Indian Ocean Ltd. and OmniScriptum S.R.L publishing group

CHAPTER I
INITIATION TO THE DESIGN OF SOFTWARE

I.1.Objectives

1. To give readers a general idea of the fundamental concepts of Software Engineering, as well as the software development and life cycle;
2. Getting to grips with UML modelling ;
3. Knowledge of the object-oriented development process for ;
4. Explain how to move from analysis to design in object-oriented programming;
5. Be able to develop software using good practice ;
6. Introduce students to working in groups on an IT project.

I.2.Prerequisites

To assimilate the course properly, students are expected to have already programmed in at least one classical language and to have knowledge of the following subjects:

✓ Classical Algorithms course.

✓ General IT courses.

✓ Course on the Computer Analysis Method with a Merise and UML approach.

✓ At least one procedural or event-based programming language such as: C, PASCAL, QBASIC and Visual Basic Net.

I.3.Notion of software quality.

In software engineering, various works have led to the definition of software quality in terms of factors that depend, among other things, on the application domain and the tools used. These include

✓ **Validity: the** ability of a software product to perform exactly the functions defined in the specifications.

✓ **Reliability or robustness: the** ability of a software product to operate under abnormal conditions.

✓ **Extensibility (maintenance):** ease with which software can be maintained, i.e. modification or extension of the functions required of it.

✓ **Reusability**: the ability of software to be reused, in whole or in part, in new applications.

✓ **Compatibility:** ease with which software can be combined with other software.

✓ **Efficiency:** Optimum use of material resources.

✓ **Portability**: ease with which software can be transferred to different hardware and software environments.

✓ **Verifiability:** ease of preparing test procedures.

✓ **Integrity**: the ability of software to protect its code and data against unauthorised access.

✓ **Ease of use:** ease of learning, ease of use, ease of data preparation, ease of error interpretation and error recovery. These factors are sometimes contradictory, and the choice of compromises must be made according to the context.

I.4. Software life cycle.

The software life cycle refers to all the stages in the development of a software product, from conception to end of life. The aim of such a breakdown is to enable intermediate milestones to be defined so that software development can be validated, i.e. that the software meets the needs expressed, and the development process can be verified, i.e. that the methods used are appropriate.

This division is based on the observation that errors are more costly the later they are detected in the development process. The lifecycle enables errors to be detected as early as possible, thereby controlling software quality, lead times and associated costs.

The software life cycle generally comprises at least the following stages following:

✓ **Defining objectives -** This stage involves defining the project's purpose and how it fits into an overall strategy.

✓ **Needs analysis and feasibility** - i.e. expressing, gathering and formalising the needs of the requester (the customer) and all the constraints, then estimating the feasibility of these needs.

✓ **Specification or design-**It is of drawing up specifications for the general architecture of the software.

✓ **Detailed design -** This stage involves precisely defining each sub-assembly of the software.

✓ **Coding (Implementation or programming) -** this is the translation into a programming language of the functionalities defined during the design phases.

✓ **Unit tests -** These are used to check individually that each sub-assembly of the software is implemented in accordance with the specifications.

✓ **Integration -** The aim is to ensure that the different elements (modules) of the software interface with each other. It is the subject of integration tests recorded in a document.

✓ **Qualification** - i.e. checking that the software conforms to the initial specifications.

✓ **Documentation -** This aims to produce the information needed to use the software and for subsequent developments.

✓ **Maintenance -** This includes all corrective actions (corrective maintenance) and developmental actions (developmental maintenance) on the software.

The sequence and presence of each of these activities in the lifecycle depends on the choice of a lifecycle model between the customer and the development team. In addition to the technical aspects, the lifecycle also takes into account the organisational and human aspects. This paper reports on a master's degree course in educational science, the aim of which was to design and produce a courseware package using HyperCard. After a brief introduction to HyperCard, theoretical information is provided on courseware and its use (typology, different models of courseware, users, teaching, etc.). This is followed by a courseware design phase, first on a mock-up, then in HyperCard. Finally, the products are evaluated using a grid. Although there is still room for improvement, this type of unit of value seems to allow a good didactic transposition from theory to practice.

NOTION ABOUT THE TUTORIAL

A tutorial (a contraction of "tutorial" and "software") can refer to two things:

✓ A computer programme used for computer-assisted instruction (CAI); more precisely, it is interactive software designed for learning knowledge (and more rarely know-how) on a given theme or subject and generally including self-assessment of knowledge; the DGLF recommends the use of the term "educational software" in the strict sense;

✓ A document (on paper or in digital format) designed to provide training in the use of software; also known as a tutorial.

The word didacticiel is a neologism that is mentioned in France Terme as being part of professional language. France Terme also recommends the term logiciel éducatif. The term exerciseur is also used when the software is based on training exercises, or an interactive multimedia environment (the activity may be free). Usage has not yet decided between these terms. It is one of the tools of information and communication technologies (ICT) and information and communication technologies for education (ICTE).We report here on the broad outlines of a value unit designed and run during the 2018-21 academic year. Part of the Masters in Education at the National Pedagogical University (UPN), this course (named TECH 2 for : TECHnologie, conception de supports éducatifs informatisés, niveau 2) allows readers, via HyperCard hypermedia software on pc, to design and produce a courseware.This course provided an opportunity to talk about CAE in a slightly different way from the usual digressions about the place of CAE in schools. Here, the theory was able to feed directly into the practice and didactic concerns of each student.This experience is not intended to be exemplary, but the reader will be able to find elements for integrating the HyperCard hypermedia production tool into the teaching context that concerns him most. Firstly, the main objectives of this course will be discussed, followed by a description and comments on how it is organised over the year. Finally, we will resituate the use of HyperCard, particularly in relation to authoring systems.

What is didactics?

The didactics of a discipline is the science that studies, for a particular field, the phenomena of teaching, the conditions for the transmission of the culture specific to an institution and the conditions for the acquisition of knowledge by a learner.

What is the purpose of general didactics?

General didactics or general methodology is a set of rules, principles and conclusions applicable to all school subjects. ... In this sense, they are concerned with the interactions between teaching and learning processes in relation to a particular school subject.

What is the purpose of general didactics?

General didactics or general methodology is a set of rules, principles and conclusions applicable to all school subjects. ... In this sense, they are concerned with the interactions between teaching and learning processes in relation to a particular school subject.

Who was the father of general didactics?
This concept was created by a Russian chemist, Vernodsky, and generalised by Father Teilhard de Chardin. It is often referred to as the didactic transposition of "knowledge".
"That's the word used.

What is general didactics?
The term general didactics implies that didactics deals with the main principles of teaching and the various ways of teaching, independently of subject content.

What is the role of didactics?
Didactics studies each stage of the learning process and highlights the importance of the teacher's role as mediator between the pupil and knowledge. The question of the relationship between knowledge and learning cannot be properly analysed without asking the question of the operational value of that knowledge.

Is didactics a science?

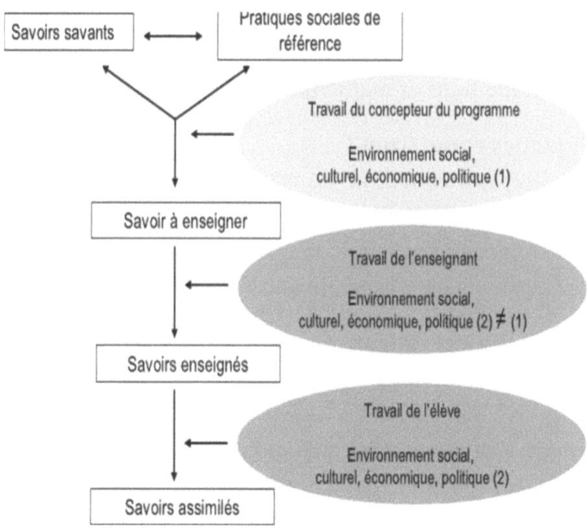

Figure 1: Didactics is a science

Didactics is a relatively young science, born in the early 1970s. Didactics does not conceive of the object of learning in a general way, but as a function of the content specific to each discipline, hence the term didactics of disciplines.

What are the characteristics of didactics?

Didactics is the study of the issues raised by the teaching and acquisition of knowledge in the various school subjects. Didactics differs from pedagogy in the central role played by subject content and in its epistemological dimension (the nature of the knowledge to be taught).

What is the purpose of language teaching?

Language didactics (LD) is the set of pedagogical methods, approaches, hypotheses and principles that enable teachers, trainers and authors of learning tools - in particular textbooks and software - to optimise the foreign language teaching/learning process.

What is the purpose of the teaching?

What is the subject of teaching, the subject taught or to be taught? Defining what is to be transmitted, what knowledge is to be constituted and how it is to be transposed is what determines the field of different didactics.24 Jan. 2011

Who is the founder of didactics?

They are Janine Rogalski and Renan Samurçay. Their early research work is clearly identified in the field of mathematics didactics.

Where does didactics come from?

Didactics, in the 1970s, was born in the wake of awakening activities at primary school level, which were then poorly defined, marking time before the place given in didactics to genetic psychology and epistemology. What is the difference between the didactic triangle and the pedagogical triangle?

What is the aim of subject didactics?

The central focus of subject didactics is the processes involved in the construction of knowledge and know-how (through transmission, reproduction or original creation) that are at work in a didactic system, i.e. in the structure made up of all the relationships that are established between the ...

What is a learning unit?

In general, a teaching unit: 1. starts from an analysis of the situation, i.e. the actual abilities and learning requirements of the pupils; ... specifies the objectives, i.e. the attitudes and knowledge that the pupils must pursue.

Objectives of the UV

✓ Choose and then break down a teaching situation so that it can be translated into computerisable sequences;

✓ Acquire the basic concepts of software ergonomics, in order to :

- Be able to design and produce a courseware package to meet these requirements;

- To be able to evaluate "off-the-shelf" courseware in this respect.

✓ To be familiar with the main HyperCard functions, and to use them to create the tutorial (programming in HyperTalk is optional, as it is difficult).

✓ Be familiar with the different types of courseware and teaching models based on CAE.

Organisation of the UV

Without going into the details of each session, I'm going to give you an overview of how the course works.

INTRODUCTION TO HYPERCARD

After a brief presentation of HyperCard's 'logic', the students try their hand at creating and manipulating the various objects available (Stacks, Cards, Buttons, Fields), following the hierarchy of complexity: from level 1 (navigation) to level 5 (author). Attractive aspects (sound effects, map changes) are also covered. It is clear that in just three two-hour sessions in groups of two, the students were not able to access all the possibilities of HyperCard, at most they were able to create a Question-Answer sequence (with the Answer command), and manipulate a few effects. These sessions were intended more to stimulate a need to study the software in greater depth, and to learn about some of its virtualities, than to provide a real grounding in programming, a grounding that would require at least twenty hours of work on a computer.

CHAPTER II

MODELLING WITH UML

2.1. Introduction

The description of object-based programming has highlighted the extent of the conceptual work required: definition of classes, their relationships, attributes and methods, interfaces, and so on. To program an application, it is not appropriate to rush headlong into writing the code: you first need to organise your ideas, document them, then organise the implementation by defining the modules and stages of the implementation. It is this process prior to writing the code that is known as modelling. its product is a model. The specifications provided by the project owner in imperative programming were often vague: as the conceptual articulations (data structures, processing algorithms) were expressed in the vocabulary of the IT department, the model often had to be developed by the latter. In principle, the object approach enables the project manager to express himself precisely using a vocabulary which, while transcribing the needs of the business, can be immediately understood by the IT specialists. In principle only, because modelling requires a level of skill and professionalism from project managers that is not currently widespread.

2.1.1. The objectives of UML

✓ Representing whole systems ;

✓ Establish explicit coupling between concepts and executable artefacts ;

✓ Taking account of scale factors ;

✓ Create a modelling language that can be used by both humans and machines, Search for a common language that can be used by all methods;

✓ Suitable for all phases of development;

✓ Compatible with all production techniques.

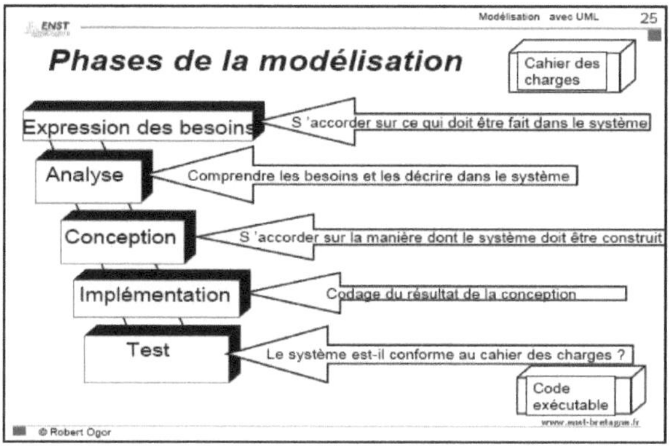

Figure 2: Modelling phases

The problem with implementing UML is simple: how do you get from the expression of requirements to the application code? UML is simply a modelling language, not a method. In fact, UML does not propose a modelling approach that explains and provides a framework for all the stages of a project, from understanding the requirements to producing the application code. A method must define a sequence of partially ordered stages, the aim of which is to produce quality software that meets users' needs within predictable timescales and costs.

2.1.2. UML is object-based modelling.

The methods used in the 1980s to organise imperative programming (notably Merise) were based on the separate modelling of data and processing. When object-oriented programming gained in importance in the early 1990s, the need for a method adapted to it became obvious. More than fifty methods appeared between 1990 and 1995 (Booch, Class-Relation, Fusion, HOOD, OMT, OOA, OOD, OOM, OOSE, etc.), but none of them managed to establish itself. In 1994, a consensus was reached on three methods:

✓ UNWTO from James Rumbaugh(General Electric) provides a graphical representation of the static, dynamic and functional aspects of a system;

✓ Grady Booch's OOD, designed for the Department of Defense, introduced the concept of a package;

✓ OOSE by Ivar Jacobson (Ericsson) is based on a description of user needs (use cases).

Each method had its advantages and its supporters. The number of competing methods had been reduced, but the risk of splintering remained: the profession could divide itself between these three methods, creating as many intellectual continents that would find it difficult to communicate.

In a considerable and almost miraculous event, the three gurus who each reigned over one of the three methods agreed to define a common method that would federate their respective contributions (they have since been nicknamed "the Amigos"). The UML (Unified Modeling Language) was born of this convergence effort. The adjective unified is there to show that UML unifies, and therefore replaces.In fact, as its name suggests, UML is not intended to be exactly a method: it is a language. Unification progressed in stages. In 1995, Booch and Rumbaugh (and a few others) agreed to build a unified method, Unified Method 0.8; in 1996, Jacobson joined them to produce UML 0.9 (note the replacement of the word method by the more modest word language). The most important players in the software world then joined the effort (IBM, Microsoft, Oracle, DEC, HP, Rational, Unisys etc.) and UML 1.0 was submitted to the OMG5. In November 1997, the OMG adopted UML 1.1 as the modelling language for object-based information systems. The version of UML currently in use in 2008 is UML 2.1.1, and improvements are ongoing.

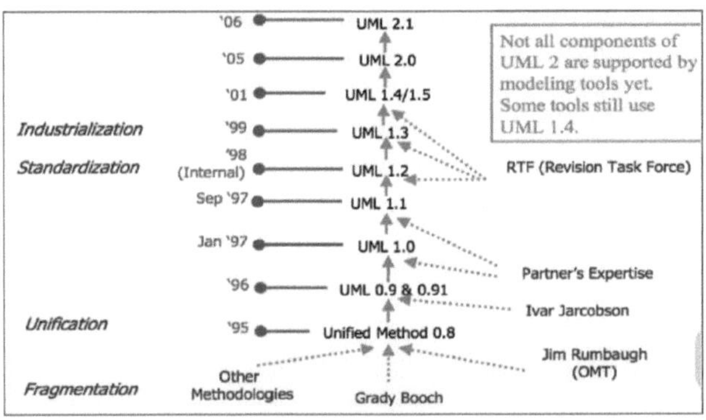

Figure 3: Different versions of UML

UML is therefore not only an interesting tool, but also a standard that is becoming the norm in object-oriented technology, and to which all the major players in the field have aligned themselves, players who have also contributed to its development.

2.2. UML diagrams

The UML comprises thirteen types of diagram, indicating as many distinct views for the representation of particular information system concepts

a. Static or structural views.

- ✓ Class diagram.
- ✓ Object diagram.
- ✓ Component diagram.
- ✓ Deployment diagram.
- ✓ Package diagram.
- ✓ Composite structure diagram.

b. Dynamic or behavioural views

- ✓ Use case diagram.
- ✓ Activity diagram.
- ✓ State machine diagram.
- ✓ Interaction overview diagram.
- ✓ Sequence diagram.
- ✓ Communication diagram.
- ✓ Timing diagram.

2.2.1. Class diagram

a. Goal

This diagram is generally considered to be the most important in object-oriented development. It represents the conceptual architecture of the system.

b. Definition

A class is an abstract (condensed) description of a set of objects in the IT application domain, taking into account their structure, behaviour and relationships.

c. Formalism

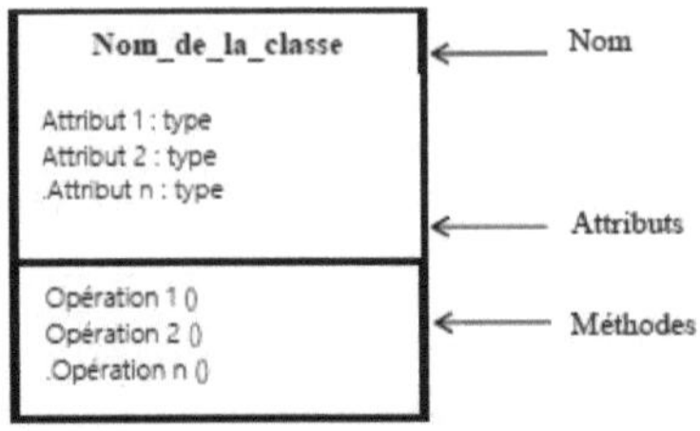

Figure 4: Formalism

d. Concepts used in the class diagram

An attribute (property)

✓ **Definition**: an attribute is a variable storing t h e set of elementary information determining the state of the object in a class.

✓ **Visibility and layout of attributes :**

The UML defines three levels of visibility for attributes:

- Public (+): The element is visible to all clients of the class.
- Protected (#): The element is visible to subclasses (or derived classes) of the class.
- Private (-):The element is only visible to objects in the class in which it is declared.

1) An object.

An object is an entity with precise boundaries that has an identity (a name). It is an instance of a class, which means that an object is a discrete entity with an identity, a state and a behaviour that can be invoked.

For example, if we consider that "**Animal**" is an abstract concept, we can say that "**Leopard**" is an instance of "**Animal**". If Animal were a class, Leopard would be an object.

2) One instance.

An instance is a concrete expression of an abstract concept. For example, the Mercedes 190 in your garage is an instance of the abstract concept Automobile.

3) An identifier.

The identifier is a special attribute which makes it possible to uniquely identify each object, an instance of the class.

4) An operation.

The operation is a functionality provided by a class representing an element of object behaviour defined globally in this class.

5) A method (or member function).

An object's method characterises its behaviour, i.e. the set of actions (called operations) that the object must perform. These operations enable the object to react to external stimuli (or to act on other objects). Moreover, operations are closely linked to attributes, because their actions can depend on attribute values, or modify them.

6) A relationship.

If there are links between objects, this translates absolutely into the relationships that exist between their respective classes.

Links between objects should be considered as instances of relationships between classes.

Here are the types of relationships between classes:

- The association.
- Generalisation/specialisation.
- Dependency.
- Interface.

2.1.1.1. The association.

✓ **Definition**: An association is a static n-ary (often binary) relationship, i.e. it links several classes together to show a structure.

✓ **Role.**

Each class participating in the association plays a role, and these roles are defined by two properties:

• **Multiplicity (or cardinality)**: this defines the number of instances of the association for one instance of the class. Multiplicity is defined by an integer or an interval of values in the reverse logic to MERISE.

1	One and only one	
0..1	Zero or one	
N or *	Several (N: natural number)	
MR.N	From M to N (M, N integers) natural)	
0..*	From zeros to many	
1..*	From one to several	

Figure 5: Multiplicity (cardinality)

Navigability has nothing to do with the direction in which the association is read, as it indicates whether an association can be traversed, i.e. whether navigability placed on a target termination indicates whether the role can be accessed from the source. By default, an association is navigable in both directions.

2.1.1.1.1. Other types of association.

- **The association class ( ) .**

An association class has the properties of associations and classes, connects to two or more classes and also contains attributes and operations.

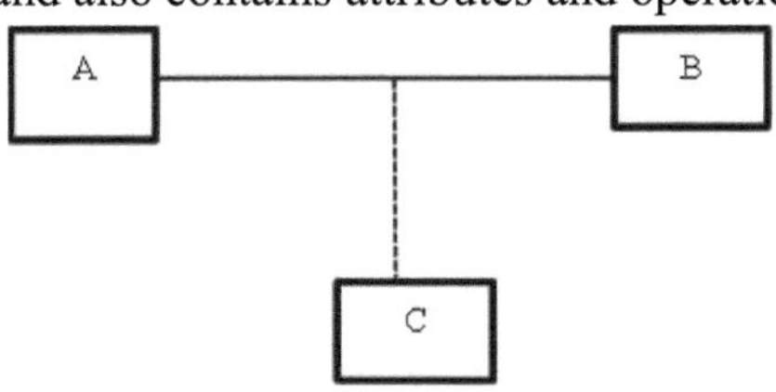

Figure 6: The association class

Note: Any association class can be replaced by an intermediate class which serves as the pivot for a pair of associations. Similarly, any association (which does not contain an attribute) involving three or more classes can give rise to a decomposition with an intermediate class.

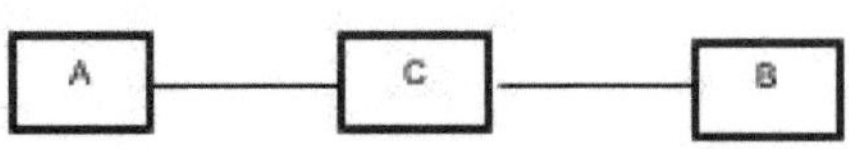

• Aggregation

Aggregation is an association that represents a relationship of structural or behavioural inclusion of an element in a set, i.e. it represents a non-symmetrical association in which one of the ends plays a predominant role in relation to the other end.

• Composition

Composition is a special case of aggregation in which the life of components is linked to that of aggregates. It describes a structural content between instances. So the destruction of the composite object implies the destruction of its components.

Figure 7: The composition

• Reflective association

Cases of reflexive aggregation can occur as soon as hierarchical relationships or kinship links are modelled.

2.1.1.2. Generalisation / specialisation ( )Δ

Generalisation describes a relationship between a general class (base class or parent class) and a specialised class (sub-class). The specialised class is completely consistent with the base class, but includes additional information (attributes, operations, associations). An object of the specialized class can be used wherever an object of the base class is authorized. In the UML, and in most object languages, this generalisation relationship is expressed by the concept of inheritance. This is also known as the inheritance relationship. Inheritance enables objects to be classified. The principle of generalisation/specialisation makes it possible to identify subsets of objects within a (generic) class (also known as a child class, derived class, specialised class, descendant class, etc.).

Generalization relations can be discovered in 2 ways:

– **Generalisation**: this involves taking existing classes that have already been highlighted and creating new classes that combine their common parts.
We need to go from the most specific to the most general.

– **Specialisation**: this involves selecting existing classes (already identified) and deriving new, more specialised classes from them, simply by specifying the differences.

Formalism and example for generalisation.

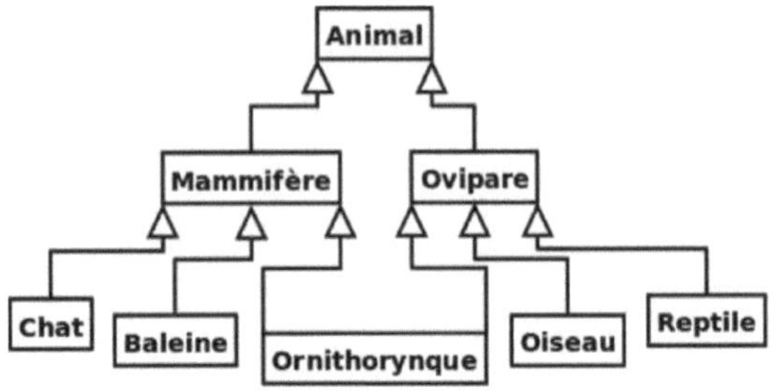

Figure 8: Formalism and example for generalisation

2.1.1.3. Dependence (--->)

Dependency relationships are used when there is a semantic relationship between several elements that is not structural in nature. A dependency relationship defines a unidirectional relationship between a source element and a target element.A dependency is a relationship between two modelling elements in which any change made to one modelling element (the influencing element) affects the other element (the dependent element).UML defines 4 types of dependency relationship. For each type of dependency, a keyword or stereotype between inverted commas can be added to the dependency relationship to specify its nature.

The 4 types of relationship are :

- **Abstraction**: which is a relationship of dependency between elements that represent the same concept at different levels of abstraction or from different points of view. Key words are: "derive", "refine", "realise", "trace".
- **Permission**: this represents a source element (package, class, operation, etc.) which has access to the destination element (package, class, operation, etc.), regardless of the latter's visibility specification. The keyword is: "friend".
- **Link**: formal parameters of a configurable class or collaboration must be linked to values. This dependency creates a link between the parameterisable class or collaboration (the target) and the parameterised class or collaboration (the source), the key word being "link".
- **Usage**: an element (source) requires the presence of another element (target) for its correct operation or implementation. The keywords are: "uses", "calls" and it represents a dependency relationship between an operation that invokes an

operation of another class.

This relationship is represented by connecting operations or classes which have these operations. The keyword is: "creates".represents the source classifier which creates an instance of the target classifier.".

Represents a dependency relationship between classifiers due to the creation of an instance of the target classifier by an operation of the source classifier. The keyword is: "instantiate".

2.1.1.4. **Interfaces**

An interface defines the visible behaviour of a class. This behaviour is defined by a list of operations with "public" visibility. No attributes or associations are defined for an interface.

An interface is in fact a particular class (with the stereotype ""interface"").

UML represents interfaces:

✓ Or by means of small circles connected by a line to the element providing the services described by the interface;

✓ Or by means of classes with the keyword "interface". This notation allows the list of interface services to be included in the operations compartment.

The possible relationships on an interface are :

- The supply

This relationship specifies that a given class provides the interface to its clients i.e. the class has this interface. A class can provide several interfaces to its clients, and each interface defines one of the class's services. This technique reduces the visibility of a class. A class that exposes its public operations exposes them to all the other classes in the model. The interface concept enables a class to define several profiles, allowing each class to use only the profile that interests it. In this way, a class can be viewed from several different perspectives, depending on which class is using it, which increases reusability.

- How it's used.

This relationship concerns any client class which wishes to access the interface class in order to access its operations. It is a standard usage relationship.

o Making it happen.

This relationship is only used for interfaces. A realization is a relationship between a class and an interface. It shows that the class performs the operations offered by the interface.

2.2.2. Use case diagram

a) Goal

This diagram is used to organise the needs of users and the corresponding objectives of a system. It focuses the expression of system requirements on its users.

b) Definition

Use cases identify the system's users (stakeholders) and their interactions with the system. They are used to classify the stakeholders and structure the system's objectives.

c) Concepts used in the user case diagram

–**Actor:** is a stereotyped type representing an abstraction that resides just outside the system to be modelled, i.e. it represents a role played by a person or thing exerting a reciprocal action with the system.

There are 4 categories of players:

- **The main players**: the people who use the system's main functions;
- **The actors secondary**: the people who perform of administrative or maintenance tasks;
- **External hardware**: the essential hardware devices which are part of the application domain and which must be used;
- **Other systems**: systems with which the system must interact.

Formalism :

He is represented by a little man with his name and his role written on it. below.

Figure 9: Actor in the shape of a man

An actor can also be represented in the form of a stereotyped filing cabinet "actor.

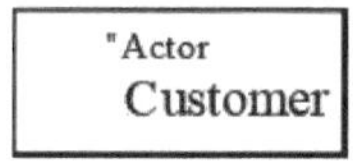

Figure 10: Actor in the form of a rectangle

Use cases

A use case is a methodical unit of externally visible functionality. It provides an end-to-end service, with a start, a continuation and an end, for the actor who initiates it. A use case corresponds to a system objective, motivated by the needs of one or more stakeholders.

Formalism :

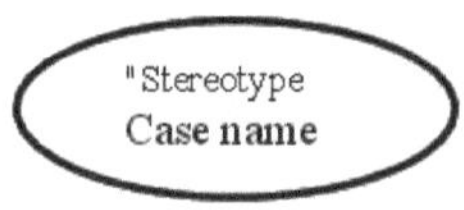

Figure 11: The use case

d) Relationships between use cases

The relationship expresses the interaction between an actor and a use case.

Formalism :

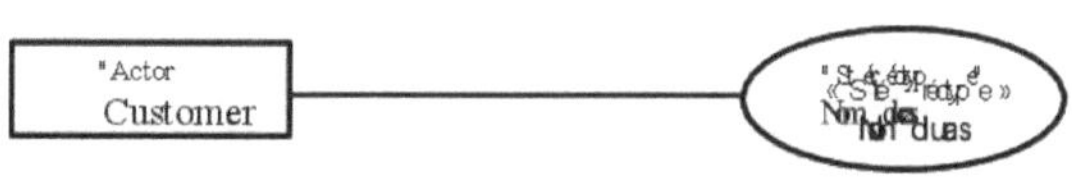

Figure 12: The interaction between an actor and a use case

Here are the three types of use case relationship proposed by UML :

▪ "include": the use case clearly and compulsorily associates another use case with the specified location,

Formalism and Example.

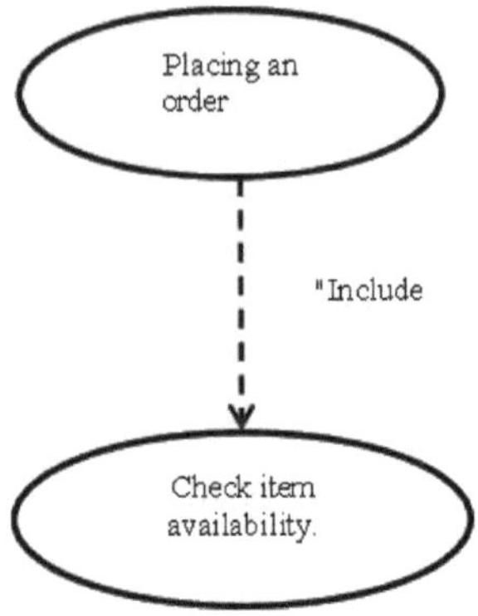

Figure 13: Use case relationship for the "Include" type

NB: To achieve the "Place an order" objective, you must "check the availability of the item".

▪ "extend": the use case implicitly and optionally inserts another use case at the specified location,

Formalism and Example

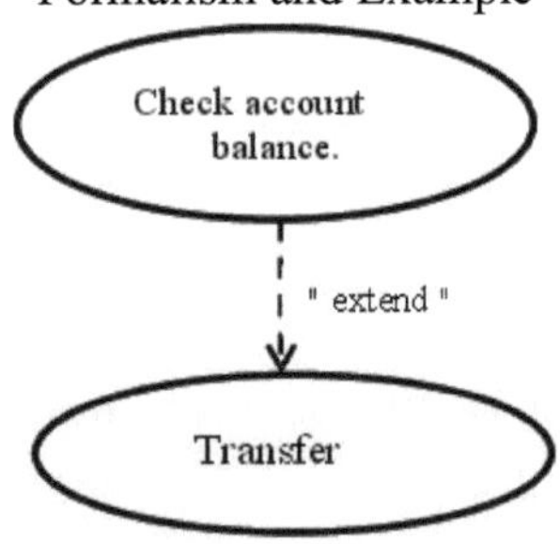

Figure 14: Extend use case relationship

▪ "Generalization: descendant use cases inherit the properties of their parent.

Formalism an example.A case A is a generalisation of a case B if B is a particular case of A. In the figure below, ordering an item via the Internet is a particular case of ordering. This generalisation/specialisation relationship is present in most UML diagrams and is reflected in the concept of inheritance in object-oriented languages.

2.2.3. State machine diagram - transitions

a) Goal

This diagram shows the different states of objects in response to events, and illustrates the scheduling of work.

b) Definition

UML state-transition diagrams describe the internal behaviour of an object using a finite state automaton. They show the possible sequences of states and actions that an instance of a class can perform during its lifecycle in response to discrete events (such as signals or method invocations).

c) Concepts used in the state-transition diagram

- **Status**

A state corresponds to a durable situation in which the objects of a class find themselves.

The symbolic representation of the states of a class of objects is as follows (rectangle with rounded edges):

Example of a report for an order :

- Preparation" status.
- In progress" status.

Predefined reports :

Two states are predefined:

- the initial state of an object: this is mandatory and unique;
- the final state: depending on the event, there may be several final states.

Initial state Final state

▪ **Event**

An event is something that happens during the execution of a system or that deserves to be modelled.

▪ **Action**

An action is an instantaneous operation that cannot be interrupted; it is associated with a transition.

▪ **Activity**

A activity is an operation of a certain duration which can It is associated with a state of an object.

▪ **Transition**

A transition is the passage from one state to another, and defines the response of an object to the occurrence of an event.

NB:

1) When an event is received, a transition can be triggered to switch the object to a new state. Events can be divided into several explicit and implicit types: signal, call, change and temporal.

2) A transition is represented by an arrow between the two states.

Formalism

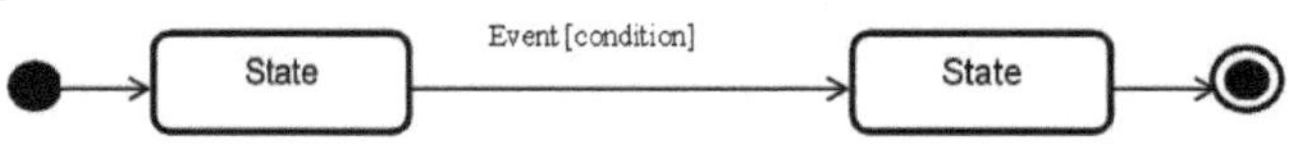

2.2.4. Activity diagram.

a) Goal

This diagram provides an overview of the progress of activities specific to an operation or use case. It can also be used to represent control flows and data flows.

b) Definition

An activity defines a behaviour described by an organised sequence of units, the simple elements of which are actions.

c) Basic concepts and general presentation

The activity diagram has a number of points in common with the state-transition diagram, as it concerns the internal behaviour of operations or use cases. However, the behaviour described here applies to control flows and data flows specific to a set of activities, rather than to a single class. The common or very similar concepts between the activity diagram and the state-transition diagram are :

Activity or control nodes.

◉ **: Final node (final state),● : Initial node (initial state),**

◇ **Decision node (choice),**

⊗ **End of flow node (exit state),→ : Transition.**

NB: The formalism remains identical for these control nodes.

✓The concepts specific to the activity diagram are :

- **Bifurcation node**

A bifurcation node (fork) enables a single incoming stream to be used to create several concurrent streams leaving the synchronisation bar.

Formalism

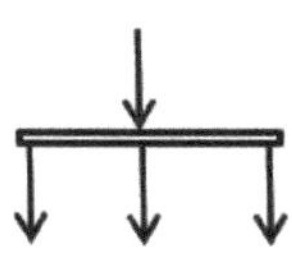

Bifurcation node (fork)

Figure 15: A bifurcation node

Example of activities with bifurcation nodes.

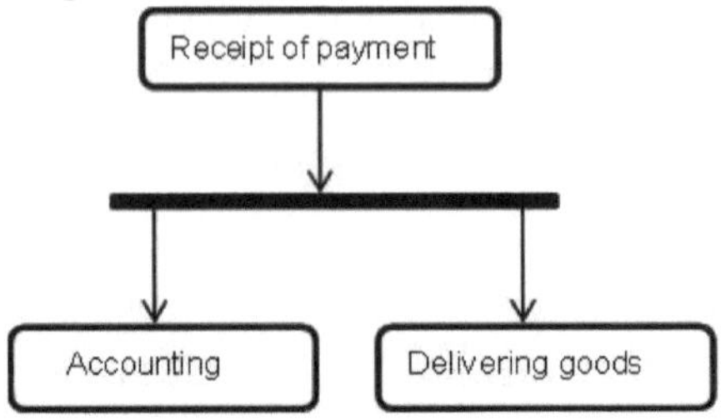

Figure 16: Activities with bifurcation nodes

- **Junction node**

A junction node (synchronisation) is used to produce a single outgoing stream from several concurrent streams at the synchronisation input. The junction node is symmetrical to the fork node.

Formalism

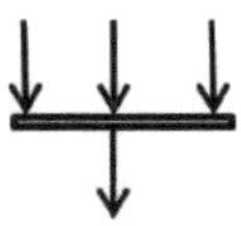

Junction node (synchronisation)

Figure 17: Junction node

Example of activities with a junction node.

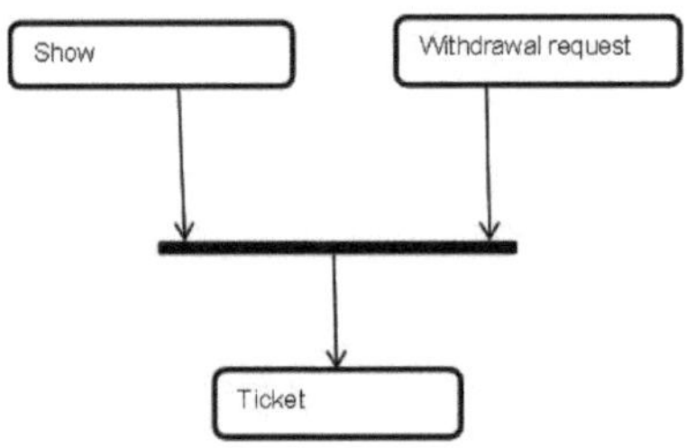

Figure 18: Activities with junction node

- **Fusion node**

A test-merge node allows several possible incoming flows and a single outgoing flow. The outgoing flow is therefore executed as soon as one of the incoming flows is activated.

Formalism and Example.

Test fusion node

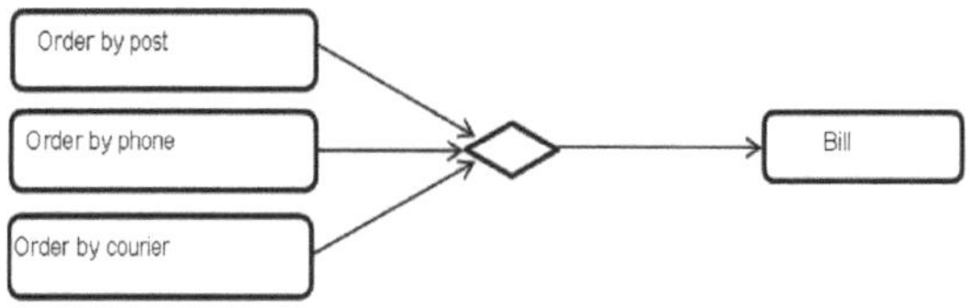

• input and output pin

An input or output pin represents a parameter which can be specified as the input or output of an action. A data name and a data type can be associated with the pin. A parameter can be of object type.

Formalism and Example.
Input or output pin

Prob1 : Integer Prob2 : Text RES : Integer

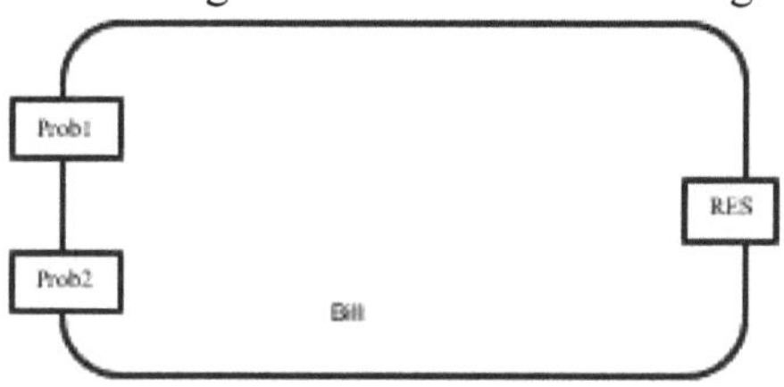

Figure 19: Input and output pins

• object flow

An object node is used to represent the flow of data between the shares.

Formalism and Example.

The data flow and object node representation formalism is given directly through an example for the command.

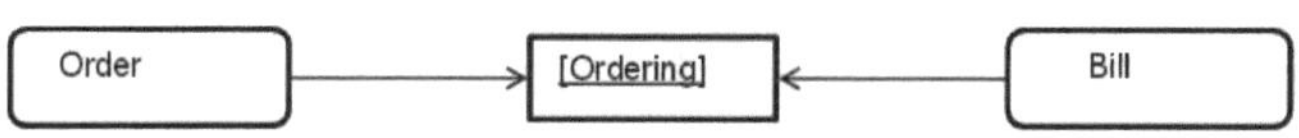

Figure 20: Object float

- **partition**

UML can also be used to organise the presentation of the activity diagram into activity lanes. Each corridor corresponds to an area of responsibility for a certain number of actions.

Object flows are also represented in the diagram. The relative order of the responsibility corridors is not significant.

- **Representation of communication actions**

In an activity diagram, as in a time diagram, communication interactions linked to certain types of event can be represented.

The types of event concerned are :

–signal,
–Time flow Formalism and Example.

Signal sent
Signal received
Acceptance of a time-related condition

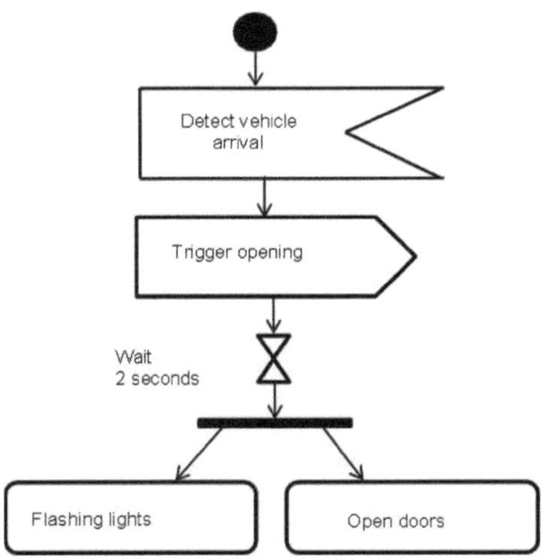

Figure 21: Communication action

2.2.5. Sequence diagram.

a) Purpose.

The aim of the sequence diagram is to represent the interactions between objects by indicating the chronology of exchanges. This representation can be done by use case by considering the different associated scenarios.

1. General presentation

The main information contained in a sequence diagram is the messages exchanged between the lifelines, presented in chronological order.

A sequence diagram is represented globally in a large rectangle with the name of the diagram at the top left, as shown in the figure below.

General formalism of a sequence diagram framework.

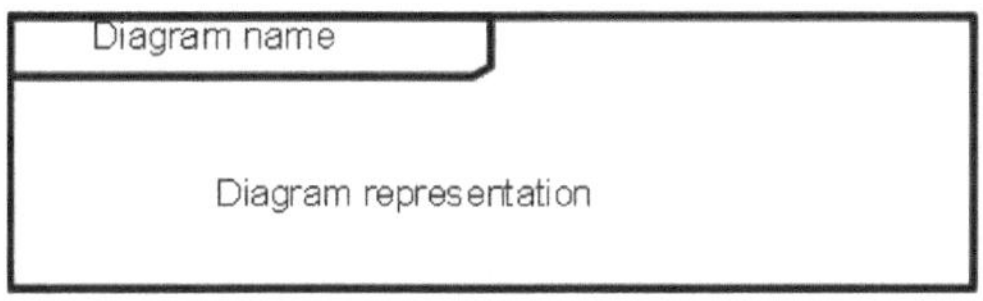

2. Basic concepts for sequence diagrams.

• Lifeline

A lifeline represents all the operations performed by an object. A message received by an object triggers the execution of an operation. Feedback can be implicit (general case) or explicit using a return message. The lifeline of objects is represented by a vertical dotted line under the symbol of the object concerned. This lifeline specifies the existence of the object concerned for a certain period of time. In general, a lifeline is represented at the full height of the sequence diagram. However, it can start and stop inside the diagram.

Formalism.

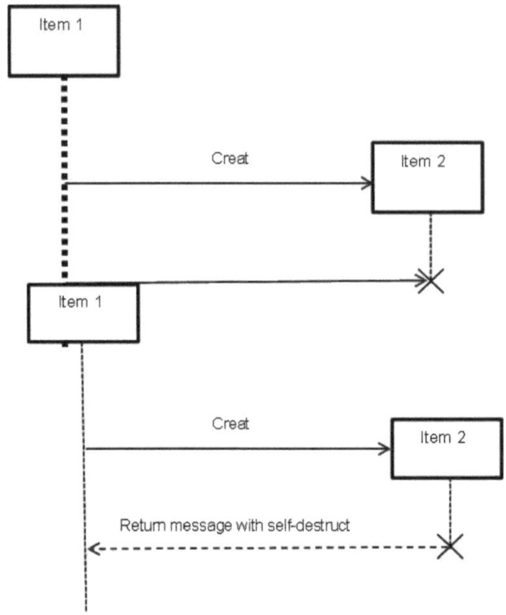

Destroy

Note: In the figures above, creation is represented by pointing the creation message at the rectangle symbolising the object created. Destruction is indicated by the end of the lifeline and a cross (X), either at the height of the message that causes destruction, or after the last message sent by an object that commits suicide.

- **Message category**

In a sequence diagram, two types of message can be distinguished:

□ **Synchronous message** - In this case, the sender waits for a response to its message before continuing with its actions. The solid-ended arrow symbolises this type of message. The return message may not be represented because it is included in the end of execution of the operation of the object receiving the message. See the figure below.

Formalism.

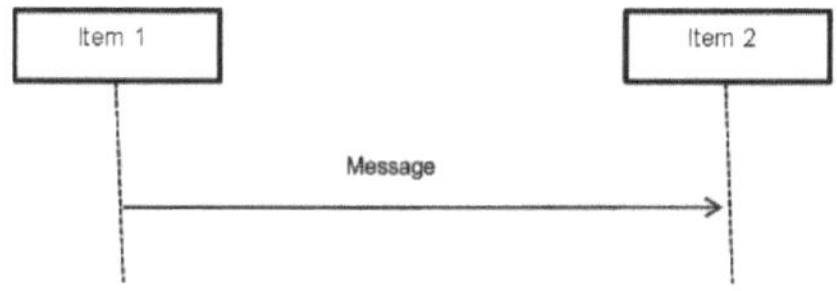

□ **Asynchronous message** - In this case, the sender does not wait for a response to its message, but continues to carry out its operations. This type of message is symbolised by an arrow with a non-full end. See the figure below.

Formalism.

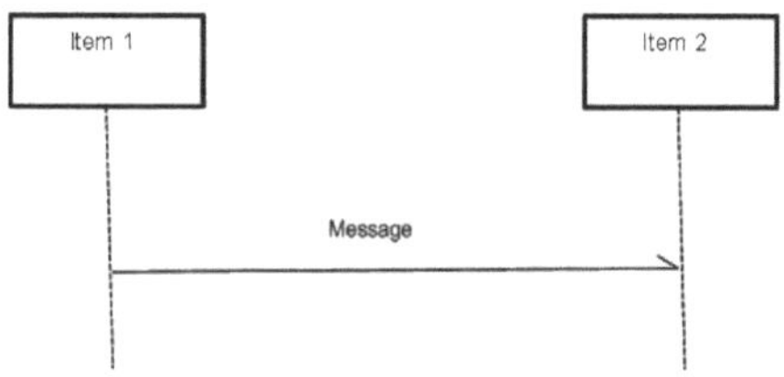

□ **Reflective message.**

An object can send a message to itself. This situation is represented by an arrow that loops back along the object's lifeline.

Formalism.

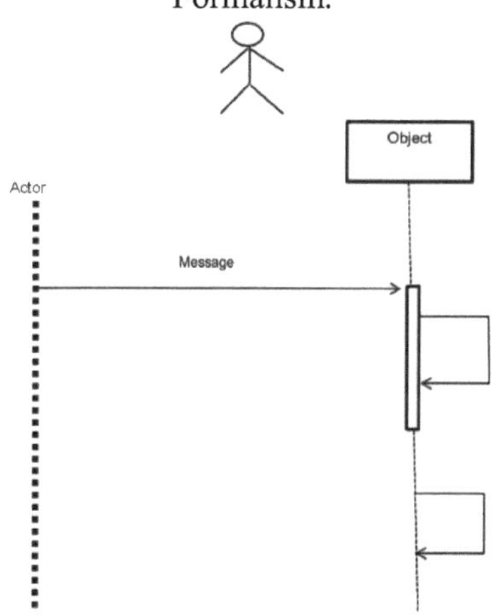

Reflective message
Another reflexive message

e. Interactions

Interaction means sending a message between objects. The sequence diagram emphasises the chronology of objects using the object lifeline.

f. Activations

Sequence diagrams are used to represent the periods of activity of objects. An activity period is the time during which an object performs an action, either directly or through another object that acts as its subcontractor.

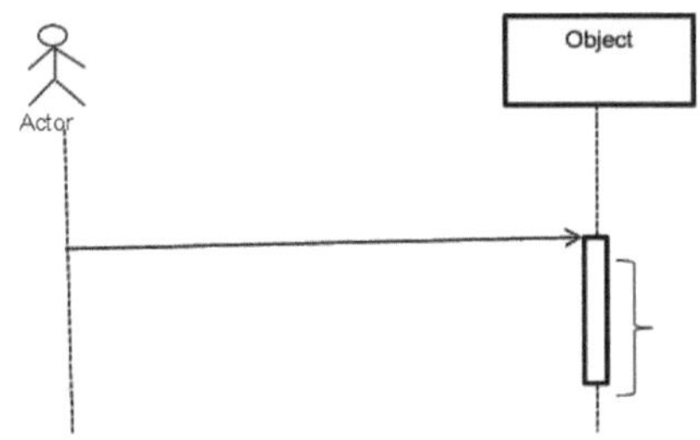

Activation time

- **Time constraint**

Timing constraints between messages can be specified. In addition, when the transmission of a message requires a certain duration, it is represented in the form of an oblique line. A general example of a time constraint is given in the figure below.

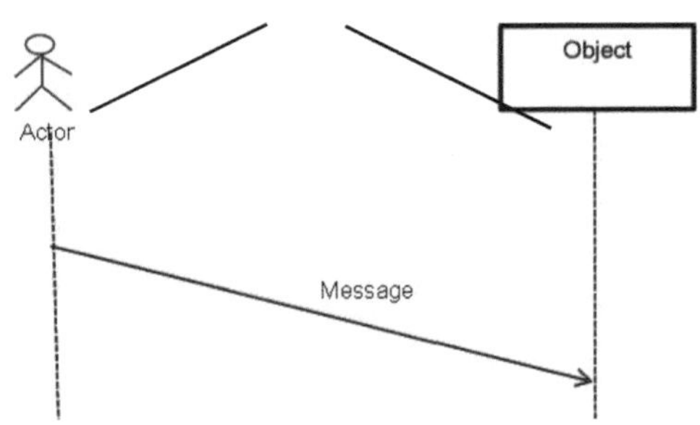

Object diagram

1. Goal.

An object diagram shows the links between objects. Objects, which are instances of classes, are connected by links, which are instances of associations. With the exception of multiplicity, which is explicitly indicated, the object diagram uses the same concepts as the class diagram. They are essentially used to understand or illustrate complex parts of a class diagram.

Formalisms and Examples.

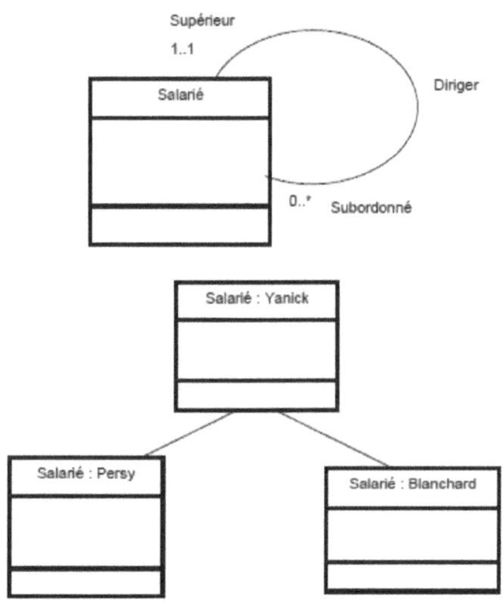

2. 4.7. Component diagram

a) Goal

The component diagram is used to represent the software components of a system and the links between these components. Software components can come from two sources: either a company's own business components or components available on the market, such as EJB, CORBA, .NET or WSDL components.

b) Basic concepts for the component diagram. A component.

A component is a physical view that represents an implementable part of a system. A component can be code, a script, a command file, a data file, a table, etc...It can implement a set of interfaces which then define the behaviour offered to other components.

A port.

A port is a connection point between a workbook and its environment, or a component port represents the connection point between the component and an interface.Graphically, a port is represented by a small square straddling the border of the workbook. The name of the port can be displayed close to its representation.

c) General component formalism.

A component is represented by a folder with the keyword "component". "You can also use a workbook with an icon representing a module in the figure below.

d) Types of representation

Two types of representation are available for model components: a "black box" representation and a "white box" representation
". For each performance, several models of components are proposed.

Black box" representation.

It is an external view of the component which presents its supplied and required interfaces without going into the details of the component's implementation. A black box can be represented in different ways.

✓ **Assembly connector**

A supplied interface is represented by a line and a small circle, and a required interface by a line and a semi-circle. These are the assembly connectors.

Formalism and Example.

An example of modelling with assembly connectors is shown in the figure below. The Command component has two supplied interfaces and two required interfaces.

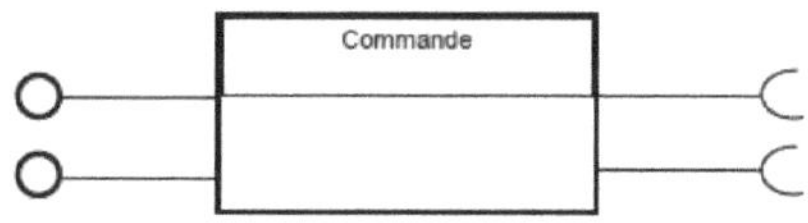

Figure 22: Assembly connector

✓ **Interface connector.**

Another representation can also be used, based on the interface dependencies uses and realises :

- for a supplied interface, this is a realisation relationship running from the component to the interface ;
- for a required interface, it is a dependency with the "uses" keyword running from the component to the interface.

Formalism and Example.

A model with interface connectors is shown in the figure below. The Ordering component has a supplied "Order Management" interface and a required "Product" interface.

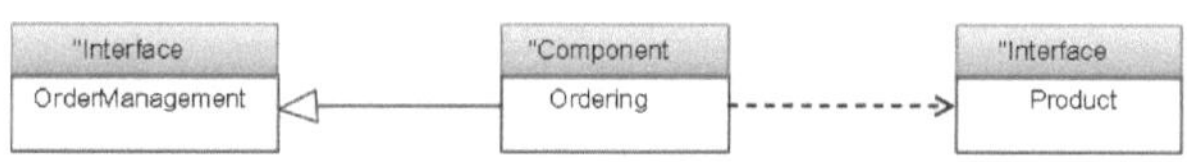

✓ **Compartment.**

A final way of modelling a component with a black box representation is to describe in text form the interfaces provided and required within a second compartment.

Formalism and Example.

A model with the compartments is shown in the figure below.

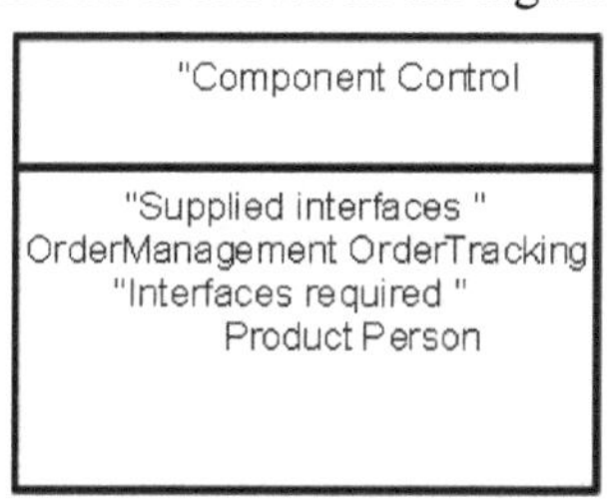

White box" representation.

It is an internal view of the component that describes its implementation using the classifiers (classes, other components) that make it up. Several models are possible for the white box representation.

✓ **Compartment**

One way of modelling a component with a white-box representation is t o describe in textual form the interfaces provided and required in one compartment, the classifiers (classes, other components) in another compartment, and the artefacts that physically represent the component in a final compartment.

Formalism and Example.

A model with the compartments is shown in the figure below.

"Component Control Control
"Supplied interfaces " OrderManagement OrderTracking "Interfaces required " Product Person
"Achievements " DetailOrder OrderLine
"Artefacts Command.dll

✓ **Dependency.**

Another internal representation of the component can also be used, using **dependencies**. In this way, the classifiers that make up the component are linked to it by a dependency relationship. Relationships between classifiers (association, composition, aggregation) are also modelled. However, if they are too complex, they can be represented on a class diagram linked to the component by a note.

Formalism and Example.

A white box model with the dependencies is shown in the figure below with the control case.

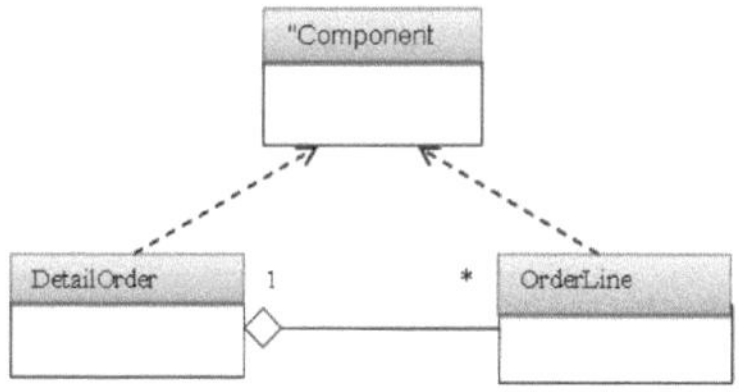

Figure 23: Dependency

2.4.8. Deployment diagram

a) Goal.

The deployment diagram represents the physical architecture supporting the operation of the system. This architecture comprises nodes corresponding to the physical media (servers, routers, etc.) and the distribution of software artefacts (libraries, executables, etc.) on these nodes. This architecture is modelled on a real network made up of nodes and connections between these nodes.

b) Basic concepts for deployment diagrams. Artefact.

An artefact is the specification of a physical element that is used or produced by the software development process or by the deployment of the system. It is therefore a concrete element such as a file, an executable or a database table.

An artefact can be linked to other artefacts by dependency links.

Formalities and examples

An artefact is represented by a rectangle in the figure below, characterised by the keyword 'artefact' and/or a specific icon in the right-hand corner of the rectangle.

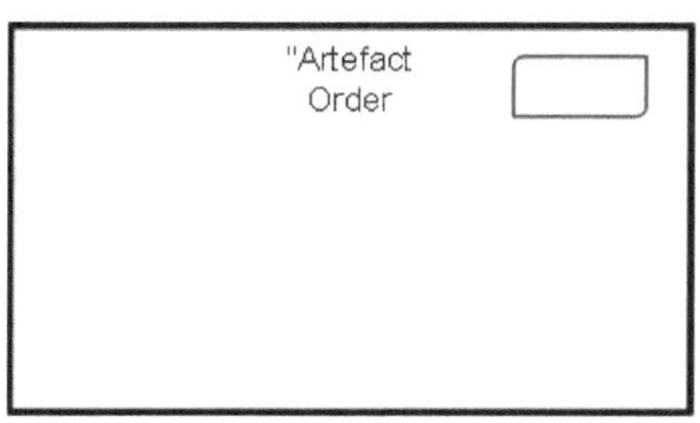

Figure 24: An artefact

Node

A node corresponds to a hardware processing resource on which artefacts will be implemented to operate the system. Nodes can be interconnected to form a network of physical elements.

Formalism and example.

A node or node instance is represented by a cube or parallelepiped as in the figure below.

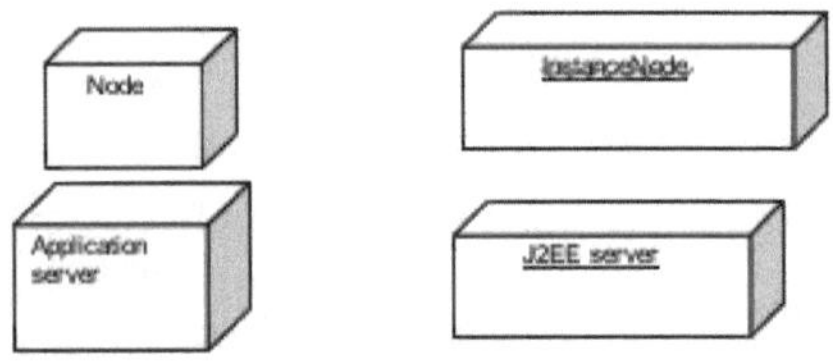

c) Links between an artefact and other elements in the diagram

There are two ways of representing the link between an artefact and its parent node:

• **Inclusive representation** - In this representation, an artefact is represented within the node at which it is physically located.

Formalities and examples

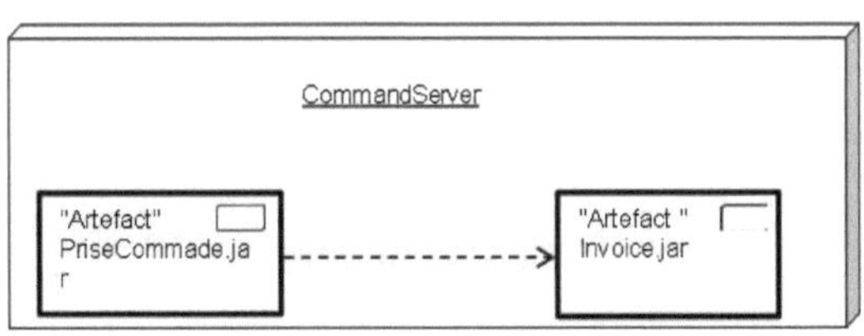

Figure 25: Links between artefacts and other elements

Representation with a "deploy" dependency link

In this case artefactis represented outside the node to which it belongs, with a dependency link between the artefact and the node typed with the keyword "deploy". Formalism and example

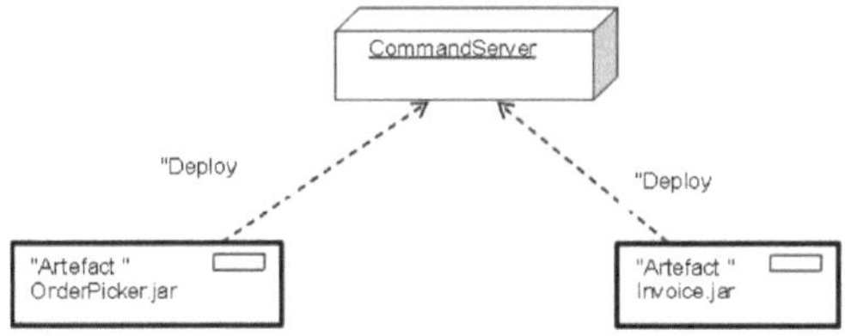

Figure 26: Representation with a "deploy" dependency link

NB: In a deployment diagram, associations between nodes are communication paths which enable information to be exchanged.

Example of a deployment diagram illustrating communication between several nodes.

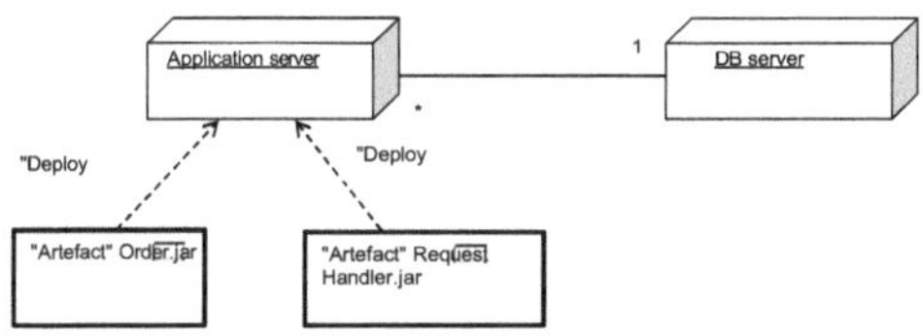

Figure 27: Deployment diagram illustrating communication between several nodes

2.4.9. Package diagram

a) Goal.

A **package** groups together modelling elements, also known as members, relating to a subset of the system. The division into packages must reflect a logical division of the system to be built, corresponding to homogeneous namespaces.

b) Please note.

The elements of a package can have visibility declared as either public (+) or private (-).

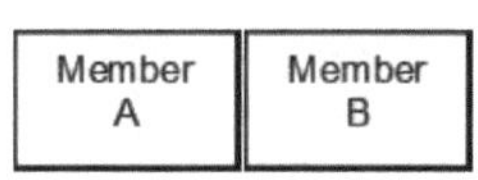

A package can import elements from another package. A package can be merged with another package.

c) Formalism

The figure below shows the general formalism of a package and the three ways of presenting a package.

✓ **Global representation** - The package name is inside the large rectangle.

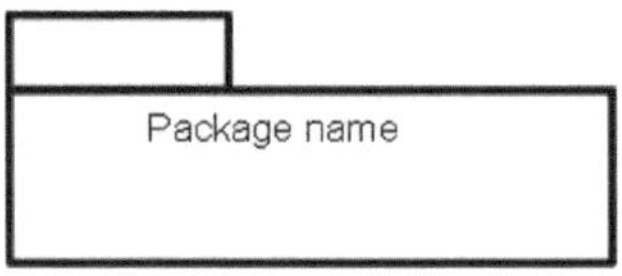

✓ **Detailed representation** - The members of the package are represented and the name of the overall package is shown in the small rectangle.

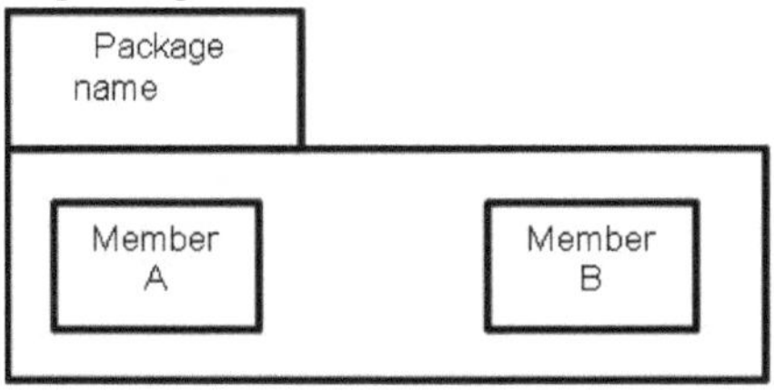

✓ **Exploded representation** - The members of the package are linked by a link connected to the package by the ⊕ symbol.

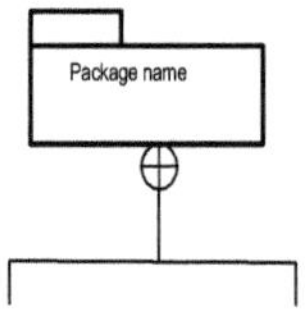

Dependency between packages

The **dependency between packages** can be qualified by a visibility level which is either public or private. The default visibility type is public. Each type of visibility is associated with a dependency link. The two types of dependency between packages are :

- **"import"** - This type of dependency allows a given package to import the namespace of another package. In this way, all the members of the given package have access to all the names of the members of the imported package, without having to explicitly use the name of the package concerned. This type of dependency corresponds to a link with "public" visibility.

• **"access"** - This type of dependency allows a given package to access the namespace of a target package. The namespace is not imported and cannot be passed on to other packages by transitivity. This type of dependency corresponds to a link with "private" visibility.

Formalities and examples

In this example, external client elements are imported into Client Domain and then into Third-Party Domain. However, the internal Client elements are only accessible via the Client Domain package and therefore not from the Third-Party Domain package.

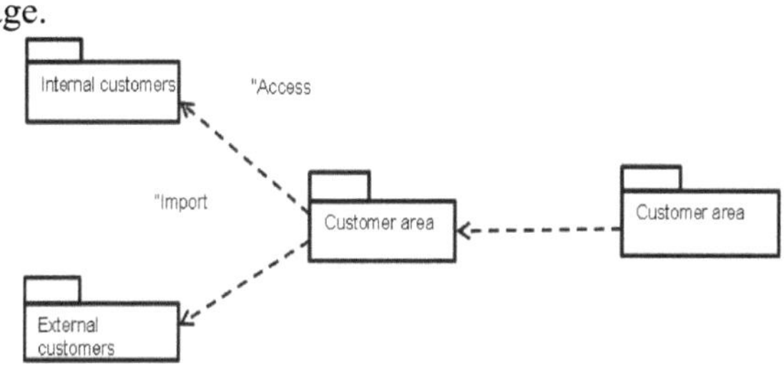

"Import"

Finally, UML also offers a merge operation between two packages. In this case, the dependency link includes the keyword "merge".

This type of link is used to merge two packages, thus obtaining a package containing the merge of the two original packages. To clarify this operation, it is important to qualify the packages involved in this merge with roles.

There are three roles to be distinguished:

• the package to be merged (entering the merge, but preserved after the merge) ;

• the receiving package (the original package before the merge, but not retained after the merge) ;

• the result package (package containing the result of the merge and overwriting the contents of the original package).

A typical example of a merge between two packages is shown in the figure below.

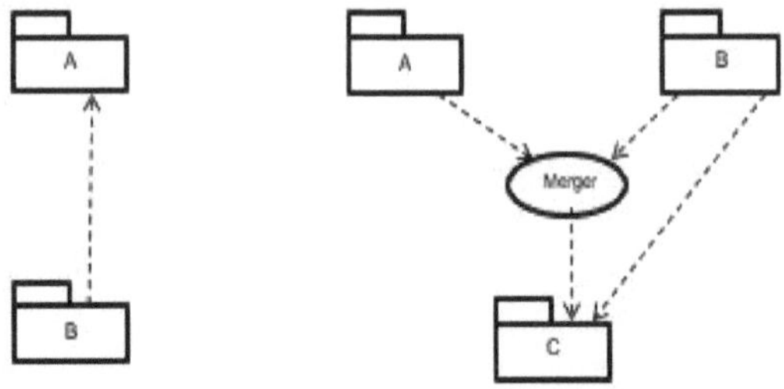

Figure 28: Merging two packages

2.4.10. Diagram of structures composite (composite structure diagram)

a) Goal

The composite structure diagram is used to describe the collaboration of instances (of classes, components, etc.) constituting particular functions of the system to be developed.

b) Basic concept Collaboration

A **collaboration** is an assembly of roles of elements that interact to perform a given function. There are two ways of representing a collaboration:

- representation through a collaboration of roles,
- representation using a composite structure: the composite structure diagram.

c) Formalisms and examples

□Représentation by collaborating on roles.

In this case, a collaboration is formalised by a dotted ellipse in which the roles of the elements interacting to achieve the desired function are shown. In this example, the Business Object Persistence function is the result of collaboration between two element roles:

- mapping: classBusiness,
- storage: tableBDD.

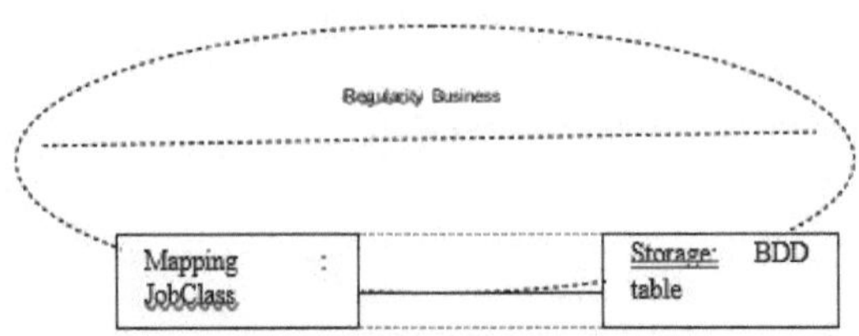

Figure 29: Role collaboration

□Représentation with a composite structure diagram.

This new representation in the figure below shows the elements of collaboration more explicitly:

- collaboration represented by a dotted ellipse ;
- elements participating in the collaboration (class, component, etc.) represented outside the collaboration ;
- the roles considered in each participation represented on the links between the participating elements and the collaboration.

BusinessCl ass		TableBDD
Attribute 1 Attribute 2 . .	Business object regularity Mapping Stockag	Attribute 1 Attribute 2 . .

Figure 30: Composite structure diagram

NOTE :

–In this example, the Business Object Persistence function is the result of collaboration between the BusinessClass class in the mapping role and the DB Table class in the storage role;
–This representation also makes it possible to specify only the attributes of the participating classes that are considered according to the roles taken into account.

2.4.11. Communication diagram

a) Goal.

The communication diagram represents interactions in a different way to the sequence diagram. The communication diagram focuses more on the spatial aspect of exchanges than the temporal aspect.

b) Basic concept.

✓ **Role**

Each participant in a message exchange corresponding to a lifeline in the sequence diagram is represented as a role in the communication diagram. A role is identified by: **<Role name>** : **<Type name>**.

One of the two parts of this identification is mandatory, as is the separator ":".

The role name corresponds to the name of the object if the actor or class has a unique role in relation to the system. The **type name** corresponds to the name of the class when objects are manipulated.

Example
Administrator: user

This example means that for a user who is seen through his administrator role.

✓ **Message**

A message corresponds to an operation call made by a sender role to a receiver role. The meaning of the message is given by an arrow above the link connecting the participants in the message (origin and recipient). Each message is identified by : **<Number>: name ( )**
More precisely, the identification o f a message must respect the syntax next:

[message no. [iteration clause] [condition]" :
"message name.

- Number of previous message received: used t o indicate the chronology of messages ;
- Message number: hierarchical message number of type 1.1, 1.2... using a letter to indicate simultaneous message transmission;
- Iteration clause: indicates whether the message is sent repeatedly. The syntax is *[iteration specification] ;
- Condition: indicates whether a condition must be met before the message can be sent.

Examples
1.2.1 * [3 times]: for a message to be sent three times in succession.
1.2a and 1.2b: for two messages sent at the same time.

Example of a message designation:
1.5e.3.3 [if t > 60]: launch ( )

This message means :

- 1.5e: number of the message received before the current message was sent.
- 3.3: current message number to be sent.
- [If t > 60]: message to be sent if t > 60.
- launch ( ): name of the message to be sent.

c) Formalisms and examples for a communication diagram

Roles correspond to objects. The link between the roles is represented by a line which is the medium for the messages exchanged. The figure below shows the basic formalism of the communication diagram.

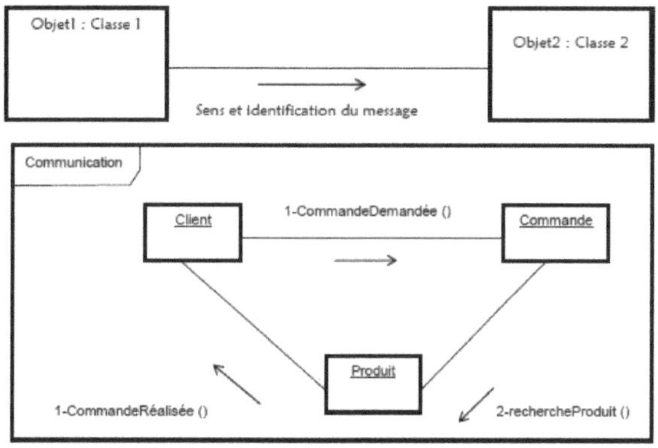

Figure 31: Communication diagram

2.4.12. Timing diagram

a) Goal.

Time diagrams can be used to represent the states and interactions of objects in a context where time has a strong influence on the behaviour of the system to be managed.In other words, the time diagram provides a better representation of changes of state and interactions between objects linked to time constraints. To achieve this, the time diagram uses the following concepts in addition to lifelines:

- Conditioned states or timelines with two possible graphical representations.
- Representations specific to temporal aspects: time scale, duration constraints, events, etc.

b) Most commonly used concepts.

The time diagram uses three basic concepts:

- **Lifeline**: this represents the object you want to describe. It is drawn horizontally. Several lifelines can appear in a time diagram.

• **Conditioned state or timeline:** the different states that the object of study can take are listed in columns, allowing you to follow the object's behaviour line by line (one line for each state).

• **Linear states:** This is the same concept as the previous one, but the succession of states is represented in a linear fashion using a special graph.

c) Formalisms and examples for a time diagram.

Or to represent the heating device of a steam iron when it is put into service according to the following rules:

- the water pump that fills the heating chamber is activated as soon as the internal water indicator shows a request;
- the water pump switches off as soon as the required water level is reached;
- the water heating system, which produces the steam, comes into action the first time the iron is used, as soon as the water level in the heating chamber is sufficient;
- the initial heating of the water lasts 3 minutes, enabling steam to be produced.

In this example, we have two objects to study: a water pump and a water heater. We will consider two significant states for each of them: activated and deactivated.

2.4.13. Diagram interaction (interaction overview diagram)

a) Goal

The global interaction diagram is used to represent a general view interactions described in the sequence diagram and control flows described in the activity diagram.

b) General presentation

The global interaction diagram gives priority to the general view of control flows in which the nodes are interactions or uses of interactions (operator ref.).

In other words, the global interaction diagram is an activity diagram in which interaction fragments or interaction uses are represented. In this way, it is possible to represent :

- choice of interaction fragments (fusion) ;
- parallel unfolding of fragments of interactions (disconnection and junction);
- interaction fragment loops.

The lifelines concerned by the global interaction diagram can be quoted in the diagram header but do not need to be represented graphically.

c) Most commonly used concepts

The global interaction diagram uses the concepts of the activity diagram, with two additions:

• Interaction fragments in the sequence diagram: As shown in the figure below, this is the notion of interaction fragment seen in the sequence diagram, but which does not need to be detailed at this level.

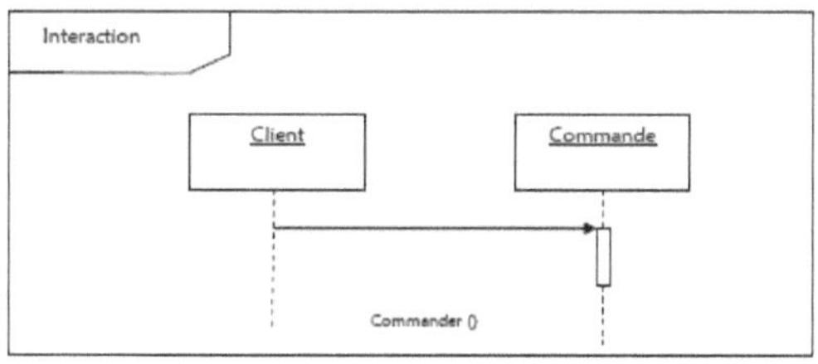

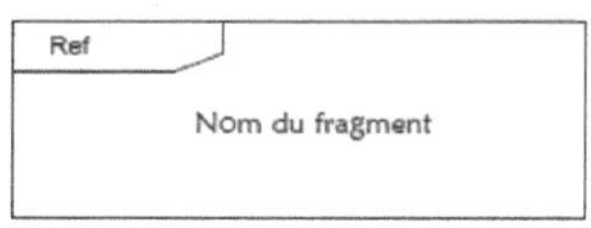

• Using interaction fragments: It is also possible to call up interaction fragments using the ref. operator, as shown in the figure below

d) Formalism and example for a global interaction diagram.

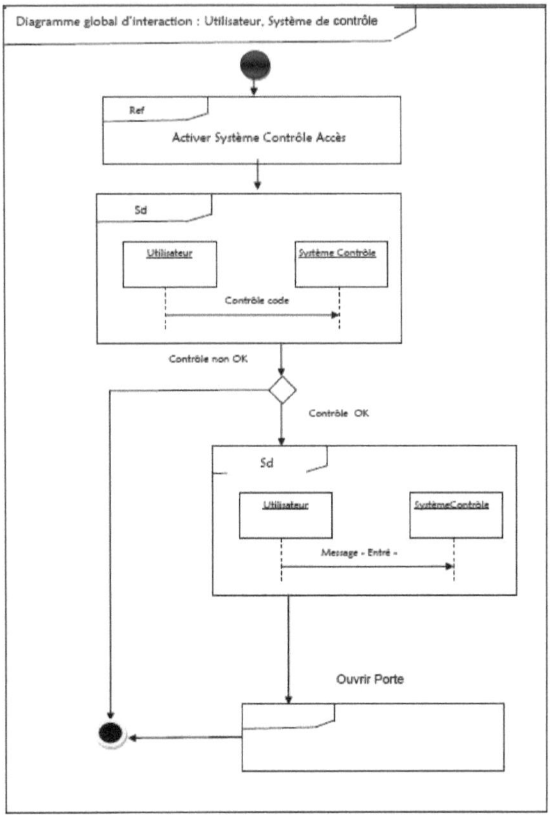

2.3. Courseware design models and methods (12 hours)

After the presentation of a typology of educational software (Mucchielli 87), the students, in groups of two, decide on the theme of their courseware project; the projects having been listed using a brainstorming exercise (Cf. § Projects). Throughout the twelve hours, the projects will be completed using the models and methods presented.To structure our discussion of CAE, we started from Depover's framework model (Depover 87), enriched by concepts developed in a more recent work (Barthet 88).

The following models are reviewed:

- of the user,
- teaching,
- of learning, of the domain (content),
- the presentation of the learning situation (software ergonomics),
- underlying the different types of educational software.

These concepts are reduced, as far as possible, to their possible transposition to HyperCard.

At the same time, the students refine the paper mock-up of their software (see § Designing HyperCard courseware screen pages). Before moving on to the production phase, the mock-ups are reviewed by each group and their feasibility checked.

2.4. Production of the tutorial.

The students create their software from the screen pages on paper. Scanning was used extensively for the illustrations. Help with script development (routines in HyperTalk programming language) is provided. In general, we refrain from commenting on the content, devoting ourselves to "troubleshooting and advice".The software produced was then tested by students in a degree course (TECH 1), using a tutorial evaluation grid (Dessus 90; Dufoyer 88).

It should be noted that not all the groups invested in this project in the same way, and we noted different levels of work, depending on the use made, or not made, of the HyperTalk language1 .

- **Level 1**: The students do not use HyperTalk programming, except to move from one card to another. Their software is of the 'page-turner' type, generally written in a single stack. Its ergonomics and presentation are, of course, rather frustrating (no user guidance, little help).

- **Level 2**: The students have developed (or adapted from manuals) small scripts to analyse answers, or to create an animation between a few cards. The tutorial is structured, with the cards divided into several piles according to their function. It generally includes a well-designed help stack.

- **Level 3**: The students have undertaken a great deal of programming work, in particular to analyse the responses and evaluate the results (scores). External routines in the public domain (Rinaldi 88) are sometimes used for sound and visual enhancement. The ergonomics and presentation are well thought out. Most of the students reinvested their knowledge in other HyperCard applications (management of an educational project, management of an experiment). They are all Macintosh owners.

2.5. Fine-tuning and evaluation.

Taking into account the evaluation and comments made by their undergraduate colleagues, the students are fine-tuning and harmonising the presentation and ergonomics of their courseware.

Then, to close the UV, a general assessment is made.

2.6. Discussion

Many authors (De Landsheere 83; Collette 90) have stressed the need for teachers to be trained in the creation of courseware, with a view to making better use of CAE.

We have tried here to show a possible avenue of research, not with an authoring language, like the authors cited, but with Hypermedia software.

This approach has a number of advantages:

- Greater courseware modularity, due to HyperCard's "object orientation", which means greater ease of design and production, and flexibility in the choice of software structure (Hennart 86).

- Possible access to a hypermedia environment (sound, scanned images, other applications, etc.);

- A wealth of presentation options, thanks in part to the previous point, but also to the Macintosh interface (multiple fonts, drawing tools) and the ability to create and manage small databases;

- It is still difficult for a non-programmer to create response analysers and note management scripts (we are working on writing buttons that integrate these functions and can be inserted into any project);

- HyperCard concepts are difficult to understand and handle (global variables, message traffic, etc.);

- The non-linearity of hypertext (Lévy 90) makes the courseware difficult to correct: a screen page has multiple predecessors, whose correct sequencing must be checked when it is corrected or created;

- The script editor is too rustic and simplistic (in version 1.1) and script execution is slow (no compilation).

The value of such a course can only be seen later, when the students try to reinvest what they have learnt in other projects, or in the choice and evaluation of 'off-the-shelf' courseware. So could HyperCard be used to train teachers in courseware design? Yes, provided that we do not put the ends at the service of the means, as Marty rightly wrote, quoted and translated by Demaizière (Demaizière 86): "Computerised materials can only be successful insofar as they are based on a teaching method that has proved successful in the classroom".

BIBLIOGRAPHY

1) (Barthet 88) M.-F. Barthet: Logiciels interactifs et ergonomie. Paris, Dunod, 1988, 219 p.

2) (Collette 90) M. Collette: Sur l'utilité d'une formation d'enseignants au dialogue élève-ordinateur. INRP. ASTER, 11, 1990, pp. 137-174.

3) (Demaizière 86) F. Demaizière: Enseignement assisté par ordinateur. Paris, Ophrys, 1986.

4) (Depover 87) C. Depover: L'ordinateur média d'enseignement. Brussels, De Boeck, 1987, 235 p.

5) (Despins 87) J-P. Despins, M-C. Bartholy: Arsenic et jeunes cervelles. Paris, U.G.E., col. 10/18, 1987, 334p.

6) (Dessus 90)P. Dessus, P. Marquet: Outils d'évaluation de logiciels éducatifs. Bulletin de l'EPI, 60, 1990, pp. 131-142.

7) (Dufoyer 88) J-P. Dufoyer: Informatique, éducation et psychologie de l'enfant. Paris, PUF, 1988, 233p.

8) (Hénnart 86) M. Hénnarrt, J-F. Berthon, M. Binse: Ecrire des logiciels pédagogiques. Paris, Cedic/Nathan, 1986, 248p.

9) (Landsheere 83) G. de Landsheere: Formation des enseignants à l'EAO: vers un contrôle de la qualité des didacticiels. Education Permanente, 70-71, 1983,pp. 73-82.

10) (Levy90) P. Levy: Les technologies de l'intelligence. Paris, La Découverte, 1990.

11) (Muchielli87) A. Muchielli: L'enseignement par ordinateur. Paris, P.U.F., Que sais-je?, 1987, 128 p.

12) (Rinaldi 88) F. Rinaldi: HyperCard: la programmation en HyperTalk. Paris, Cédic/Nathan, 1988.

TABLE OF CONTENTS

More Books!

yes

I want morebooks!

Buy your books fast and straightforward online - at one of world's fastest growing online book stores! Environmentally sound due to Print-on-Demand technologies.

Buy your books online at
www.morebooks.shop

Kaufen Sie Ihre Bücher schnell und unkompliziert online – auf einer der am schnellsten wachsenden Buchhandelsplattformen weltweit! Dank Print-On-Demand umwelt- und ressourcenschonend produzi ert.

Bücher schneller online kaufen
www.morebooks.shop

info@omniscriptum.com
www.omniscriptum.com

OMNIScriptum

MIX
Papier aus verantwortungsvollen Quellen
Paper from responsible sources
FSC® C105338

Printed by Books on Demand GmbH, Norderstedt / Germany